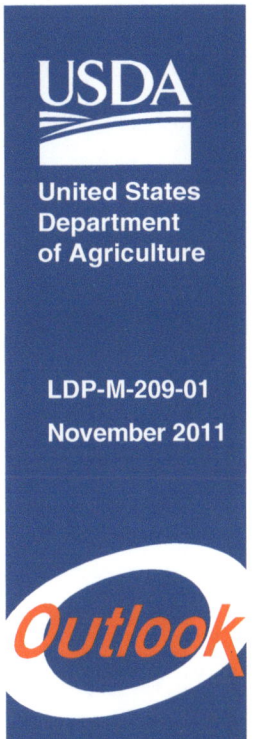

United States Department of Agriculture

LDP-M-209-01
November 2011

Contents

Introduction 2
What Are Animal
Byproducts? 3
Byproduct Production 6
Byproduct Values 10
Foreign Byproduct Price
Comparison. 15
U.S. Edible Offal and the
Global Marketplace 17
Conclusions 24
References 25
Appendix A—Types of
Offal by Category 28
Appendix B—Steer
Byproducts Model 29

Approved by USDA's
World Agricultural
Outlook Board

A Report from the Economic Research Service

www.ers.usda.gov

Where's the (Not) Meat?
Byproducts From Beef and Pork Production

Daniel L. Marti, dmarti@ers.usda.gov
Rachel J. Johnson, rjohnson@ers.usda.gov
Kenneth H. Mathews, Jr., kmathews@ers.usda.gov

Abstract

Animal byproducts contribute to the bottom line of the U.S. meat industry. Byproducts (edible offal (including variety meats), inedible offal, hides and skins, blood, fats, and tallow) include all parts of a live animal that are not part of the dressed carcass and constitute about 30 percent of the liveweight of hogs and about 44 percent of the live-weight of cattle. Byproducts from animal slaughter provide raw materials used in pharmaceutical, cosmetic, household, and industrial products. Exports of edible offal also contribute to the value and profitability of the U.S. meat processing industry in a way that leads to higher prices for livestock producers, as byproducts account for more than 23 and 35 percent of the volume of beef/veal and pork exports, respectively. Regression analysis indicates that a 10-percent increase in the steer byproduct drop value adds a 1-percent increase in the five-area weighted average price for all grades of steers. U.S. exports of beef/veal and pork edible offal have increased in recent years, mostly due to population growth, income growth, and consumer preferences for variety meats, especially in Asia. Income growth in the global marketplace, however, may have varied effects on the consumption and trade of variety meats.

Keywords: animal byproducts, offal, edible, inedible, variety meats, hogs, cattle, trade

Acknowledgments

The authors gratefully acknowledge the reviews of Erin Daley Borror, Thad Lively, Paul Clayton, Kevin Smith, and Courtney Heller of the U.S. Meat Export Federation; Claire Mezoughem and Lesley Ahmed of USDA's Foreign Agricultural Service; Sherry Wise, Warren Preston, Martin O'Connor, and Bucky Gwaltney of USDA's Agricultural Marketing Service; Herbert Ockerman of Ohio State University; Richard Stillman, William Hahn, Mildred Haley, and Molly Garber of USDA's Economic Research Service (ERS); and Shayle Shagam of USDA's World Agricultural Outlook Board. The authors would also like to acknowledge Fred Gale of ERS for gathering and translating Chinese pork prices and Ron Plain of the University of Missouri for providing historical carcass weight data. The authors appreciate and acknowledge the editorial and design assistance of John Weber and Victor B. Phillips, Jr. of ERS.

Introduction

Animal byproducts, or offal, may not make up the real "heart" of the U.S. meat industry, given that the multiple uses for inedible animal byproducts are not often considered. And, variety meat dishes, such as beef tongue or pig heart, do not typically grace Americans' dinner tables. Nonetheless, offal derived from beef and pork slaughter contributes to the bottom line of the U.S. meat industry. During 2001-10, edible animal byproducts (byproducts that do not include hides and other inedibles) averaged 23-35 percent of the volume of U.S. pork and beef/veal exports and 14-19 percent of the value.

Animal byproducts include all parts of a live animal that are not part of the dressed carcass. Produced jointly in the process of harvesting meat from the animal, byproducts constitute an estimated 30 percent of the liveweight of hogs and about 44 percent of the liveweight of cattle. In the United States, animal byproducts fall into three categories: hides, inedible offal, and edible offal, with variety meats being a subcategory of edible offal. Based on live value, byproducts account for more than 10 percent of the value for cattle and more than 6 percent of the value for hogs. Tallow accounts for about 20 percent of the value of live cattle, and lard accounts for about 9-17 percent of the value of a live hog. Although hides/skins and rendered products contribute to the value of cattle and hogs, this report focuses primarily on offal products. Hides account for 30-75 percent of the byproduct drop value for cattle but very little of the drop value for hogs.[1]

The use of animal byproducts dates back to early civilization, with hides used for clothing and intestines used for food containers. The first recorded use of a cleaning compound, a soap made from animal fat and lye, was in the first century A.D. Early U.S. history also records production and uses for hides and tallow in the Western United States (Ockerman and Hansen, 2000).

Animal byproducts provide many of the raw materials used to make pharmaceutical, cosmetic, household, and industrial products. These products, along with hides and well-known variety meats, such as liver, tongue, hearts, and feet, all add value to the U.S. meat industry. But just how important are they and what role do they play in export trade?

[1]The drop value reflects the wholesale price that packers receive from the animal's byproducts that "drop" off an animal's carcass when it is dressed, on a dollar per hundredweight basis.

What Are Animal Byproducts?

U.S. consumers have come to depend on the wide array of products made from animal byproducts (see app. A). Among countries, the product mixes comprising the edible and inedible offal categories can vary slightly but are mostly consistent. Inedible animal byproducts—those typically considered or mandated as not edible—are the primary raw materials used in the manufacture of a broad assortment of industrial, household, cosmetic, pharmaceutical, and medical supplies, in addition to such products as lubricants, plastics, soaps, glycerin, and gelatins (Aberle et al., 2001). In addition to having domestic value, edible offal contributes as much as one-fourth of the volume of U.S. beef exports and one-fifth of the volume of U.S. pork exports (Marti and Johnson, 2010).

Inedible Byproducts

Inedible animal byproducts include hide or skin, hair, horns, teeth, fats, bone, ligaments and cartilage, feet, glands, blood, and lungs. Although the share varies among individual animals, cattle hides account for about 75 percent of the byproduct value of a beef animal, much more than pork skins contribute to the value of a hog. U.S.-produced hides are often exported to China, Hong Kong, South Korea, Taiwan, Mexico, and the European Union, where they are tanned and processed into leather for shoes, purses, clothing, car seats, and other items.

Some inedible offal, along with normally edible offal that has been deemed unsuitable for human consumption, bones from meat processing, and cattle that are unsuitable for human consumption (nonambulatory and other condemned cattle), is rendered for use in the industrial, cosmetic, and feed manufacturing industries. Processors render products by heating animal tissues and skimming off the fats and oils. Both the skimmed fats and oils and the residual materials are converted to materials that have economic value, generally as inputs into further manufacturing processes. Rendering also helps minimize the release of animal tissues into the environment as potential biological hazards (Aberle et al., 2001; Danilevici et al., 2009). According to Prokop (1996), about 40 percent of the weight of a live beef animal goes through the rendering process. Rendered meat and bone meal is a valuable source of protein in pig and poultry feed, pet foods, and even fertilizer. The use of meat and bone meal made from cattle and sheep (and other ruminants), however, is restricted by regulations designed to reduce the risk of bovine spongiform encephalitis (BSE) (see Mathews, 2008; Mathews et al., 2006).

Animal byproducts also are important to the development and ultimate availability of modern human medicines. Glands removed from livestock at slaughter, such as the adrenal, parathyroid, pituitary, thyroid, and thymus glands; ovaries; pancreas; and testes provide many of the hormones and enzymes used in the medical field (Aberle et al., 2001). Among the medicines that can be obtained from animal glands are epinephrine, estrogens, progesterone, insulin, trypsin, parathyroid hormone, adrenocorticotropic hormone (ACTH), somatotropin, thyroid stimulating hormone, testosterone, thyroxin, and thymosin. Serums, vaccines, antigens, and antitoxins are also derived from many food-animal tissues acquired both during slaughter and processing of the animal (Pearl, 2005). Purified animal blood is fractionated into numerous products, including thrombin, used for blood coagulation agents and skin-graft procedures; fibrin, used in surgical repair of internal organs; and fibrinolysin, used to help heal minor burns or as a wound-cleaning agent.

Certain parts from pigs and cattle are used for xenotransplantation, the insertion of tissue from one species into another. Skin, brain cells, insulin, heart valves, and lungs from pigs are all used for human transplants as well (Goodlight, 2010). Pig skins are used for initial treatment for burn patients, while bone cartilage and bone fragments are used as substitutes for diseased or damaged human tissue parts (Pearl, 2005). Intestines provide surgical ligatures; blood provides albumen, amino acids, fetal serum, and thrombin; bones provide calcium and phosphorus; and other inedible offal provides liver extracts, bile extract, cortisone, heparin, cholesterol, rennet, and pepsin. In many of these treatment uses, no other synthetic products function or perform equally well. In other cases, the extracts of animal byproducts have provided the scientific basis for the development of synthetic substitutes, such as insulin and other pharmaceutical products (Pearl, 2005).

Animal byproducts are also a major contributor to the growth and expansion of the pet food industry (Corbin, 1992). Animal byproducts in pet food diets are good sources of digestible protein, fat, vitamins, and minerals and, historically, have supplied the majority of these nutrients for pets. For example, animal byproducts account for 25-40 percent of the dry matter in premium dog diets (Murray et al., 1997).

Edible Byproducts

The edible byproducts from slaughtered animals are segregated, chilled, and processed. These products include livers, hearts, tongues, tails, kidneys, brains, sweetbreads (the thymus and/or pancreas gland, depending on an animal's age), tripe (stomach), melt (spleen), chitterlings and natural casings (intestines), fries (testicles), rinds, head meat, lips, fats and other trimmings, blood, and certain bones. Typically, edible byproduct yield is around 12 percent of liveweight from cattle and about 14 percent of liveweight from hogs when pork rinds are included (Ockerman and Hansen, 2000, pg. 23).

Edible byproducts can be categorized into variety meats or edible fats and oils. Edible organs and glands—brains, hearts, kidneys, livers, melts, sweetbreads, tongues, and chitterlings—along with oxtails are categorized as variety meats and are usually sold with minimal processing. Intestines and cheek meats are usually processed further, often into sausages and other processed meat products. Extra trimmings and tails are used in soups and bouillons; extra trimmings, blood, stomachs, and intestines can be sausage ingredients or casings. Certain stomach parts also provide rennet for cheese making. Gelatin is used in such products as ice cream and jellied foods and is produced in part from bones and skins (Aberle, 2001).

While many of the variety meats are typically fatty and higher in cholesterol, they are also good sources of essential vitamins and nutrients:

- Livers are high in vitamin A, iron, zinc, B vitamins, vitamins C and D, copper, and fatty acids.
- Hearts contain large amounts of iron and are a good source of selenium, zinc, phosphorous, niacin, and riboflavin, but they are very low in sodium.
- Brains are rich in niacin, phosphorus, B_{12}, and vitamin C.
- Tripe contains abundant protein and B_{12}.
- Sweetbreads are very high in vitamin C.
- Kidneys are high in protein and contain riboflavin and niacin.
- Tongues are a good source of B_{12} but are low in sodium.
- Hog feet are low in sodium but are a good source for selenium.

In some countries, variety meats are considered delicacies and are the basis for many traditional dishes; in other countries, their consumption is associated with low-income populations (Halstead, 1999). Demand for variety meats is especially strong in many Asian nations. In China, many recipes call for sharp-tasting variety meats rather than muscle cuts, which are considered bland (Hayes, 1997); cow tongues are considered expensive delicacies in Japan; and sliced beef feet are used for soup in South Korea. Tongue and liver are used in many Mexican dishes, such as putzaze (tripe and liver with tomatoes), lengua (tongue with green chilies), and menudo norteña (tripe soup). In Russia and Egypt, two of the world's leading importers of edible offal (head meat, liver, heart, kidney, and tongue), variety meats are more commonly consumed by lower income households and are used as an inexpensive way to obtain high-quality protein and nutrition (Kamenski, 2006).

Byproduct Production

Estimates of total U.S. byproduct production by species are not publicly available, although limited data are available from the U.S. Department of Commerce and *Render Magazine* (National Renderers Association) for some fats and oils and other rendered products from all species. USDA's Agricultural Marketing Service (AMS) also reports data in its *Pork and Beef Variety Meats Report* on the number of 40,000-pound loads of various byproducts that are sold each month as well as the average value and weight of many of these specific items. The items detailed in the AMS report include only those sold directly for human consumption or those sold to multiple companies. Thus, recorded byproduct levels may not be consistent with potential quantities because the data do not cover byproducts sold exclusively to one company for the production of a specialty product.

The data gathered from AMS can be used to estimate the total volume of beef and pork variety meats produced in the United States (see fig. 1). AMS data are the only production numbers that reflect actual counts and not estimates. This information, however, is provided voluntarily and may therefore represent only a portion of the byproducts harvested from hogs and cattle.

Another way to determine the volume of animal byproduct production is to create an "upper-bound" estimate using available data sources. A comparison of byproduct quantities reported voluntarily and byproduct quantities estimated by ERS provides evidence of the discrepancy between potential and reported amounts in the manufacturing sector. Ockerman and Hansen (2000) suggest that animal byproduct volumes can be estimated from slaughter numbers and dressing percentages. In addition to shrinkage losses, more than 2 percent of the carcass weight is often unaccounted for (Ockerman and Hansen, 2000). Confidential sources in academia and the packing and processing sectors reveal that byproducts collected from livestock can vary

Figure 1
Reported U.S. monthly beef and pork byproduct production from AMS data

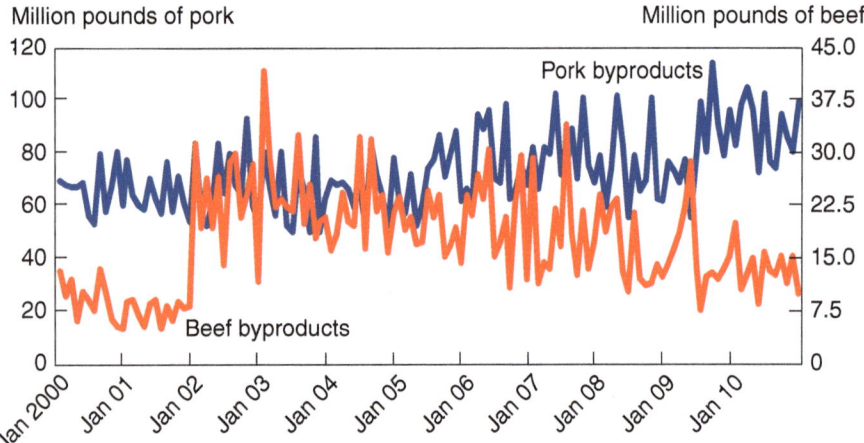

Note: Data are calculated by multiplying the total number of loads of delivered offal and byproducts of beef or pork recorded by AMS by 40,000 pounds, the weight of a standard load.
Source: USDA, Economic Research Service using data from USDA, Agricultural Marketing Service (AMS).

from animal to animal, packer to packer, and over time, making it difficult to determine the exact byproduct amount produced at any time.

ERS estimates are based on data on the number of head slaughtered for each respective species from USDA, National Agricultural Statistics Service's *Livestock Slaughter* and assessments gathered from scholarly literature on animal byproducts. By subtracting both the weight of muscle cuts and trimmings sold at the retail level and the estimated shrink and other waste loss (stomach contents, water, etc.) from the live weight of the animal, it is possible to estimate an upper bound for potential byproduct production. It is also worth noting that some fat and bone that typically remain on the carcass at slaughter and are later removed also contribute to byproduct production. These estimates may be conservative because the numbers do not include condemnations that are rendered and added to the inedible byproducts market. Data from the literature reveal that about 11 percent of a typical slaughter hog's liveweight is lost through shrinkage or waste or is somehow unaccounted for (Aberle et al., 2001). After fat and bone have been trimmed off, about 77-79 percent of a dressed hog carcass weight produces muscle meat cuts and trimmings sold at the retail level (Aberle et al., 2001; USDA, ERS, 1992). The remaining share serves as an estimate of the total byproducts (volume) produced per hog. For cattle, about 14.1 percent of a typical steer's liveweight is lost through shrinkage or waste or is otherwise unaccounted for (Aberle et al., 2001; Duewer, 1998). After fat and bone have been trimmed off, about 69-70 percent of a dressed steer carcass weight produces muscle meat cuts and trimmings sold at the retail level. The remaining share serves as an estimate of the total volume of byproducts produced per steer.

Time series data reveal that total annual production of beef byproducts has remained fairly constant over the last decade or so, starting at about 18.5 billion pounds in 1997 and growing to almost 19 billion pounds in 2010 (fig. 2). Although estimates in other studies may include veal byproducts with beef byproducts, this analysis does not because, at most, veal byproducts add only one-half of 1 percent to total volume of beef offal production. The same

Figure 2
Estimated monthly red meat byproduct production

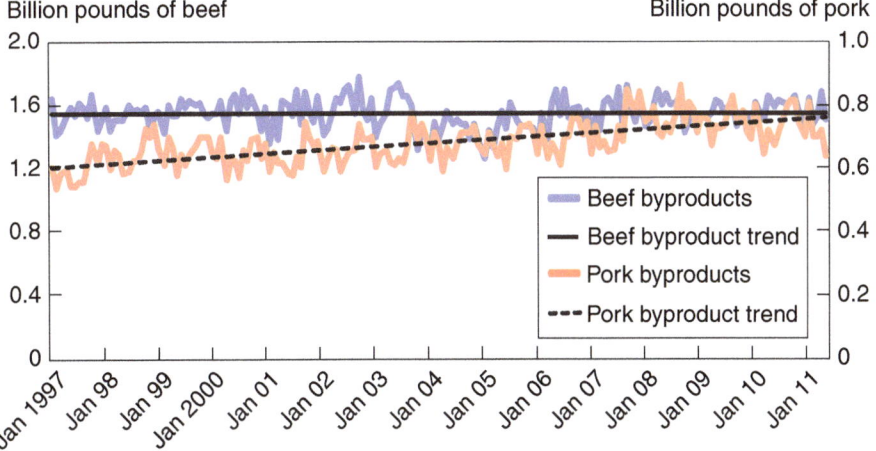

Source: USDA, Economic Research Service compiled from USDA, National Agricultural Statistics Service; Ockerman and Hansen, 2000; and Aberle et al., 2001.

Figure 3
Estimated beef byproduct production
Billion pounds

[Line chart showing Retail cuts, Retail cut trend, Byproducts, and Byproduct trend from 1921 to 2006, with values rising from about 0.3 billion pounds in 1921 to about 2.0 billion pounds by 2006.]

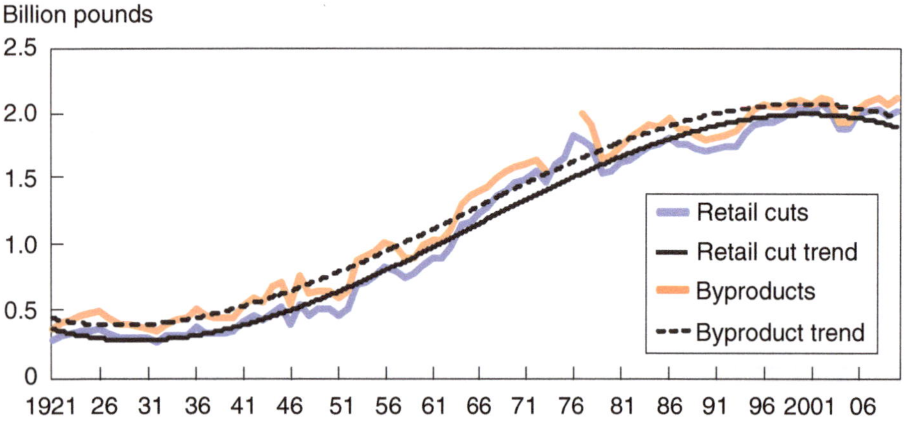

Note: Due to gaps in live weight data from 1974-76, we were unable to provide a continuous set of byproduct production data.
Source: USDA, Economic Research Service using data from USDA, National Agricultural Statistics Service; Ockerman and Hansen, 2000; and Aberle et al., 2001.

time series data show that U.S. production of pork byproducts has grown over the last decade, much like the pork industry itself. Annual production of pork byproducts rose from about 7.1 billion pounds in 1997 to about 8.9 billion pounds in 2010.

Beef byproduct production is highly correlated with beef production (see figure 3). In 1921, only 38 percent of the liveweight of federally inspected cattle was sold at retail as muscle meat cuts and ground meat, and 48 percent of the animals' weight was available for production as beef byproducts. By 2010, these percentages were nearly equal: 42 percent of the animals' liveweight was used to produce retail muscle and ground meats, and 44 percent was available for byproduct production. This change is attributed to a shift in cattle genetics motivated by consumer preferences for more meat and less fat.

Pork meat production and pork byproduct production are also highly correlated. In 1921, 44 percent of the liveweight of federally inspected hogs was used as muscle cuts and trimmings meat and about 45 percent was available for production as pork byproducts. Historical data on dressed weights from USDA's National Agricultural Statistics Service included back fat in the carcass weight until the late 1950s. Therefore, this analysis adjusts the data to extract fat from dressed weights prior to their separation in the USDA data to reflect a more homogenous dataset (Plain, 2010) (see fig. 4). As hog fat and lard became less valuable beginning in the 1960s, the hog industry began breeding animals to meet the evolving demand for leaner animals with more muscle content. By 2010, 59 percent of the hog's weight produced retail muscle and trimming meat and only 30 percent was available for byproduct production.

Figure 4
Estimated pork byproduct production

Billion pounds

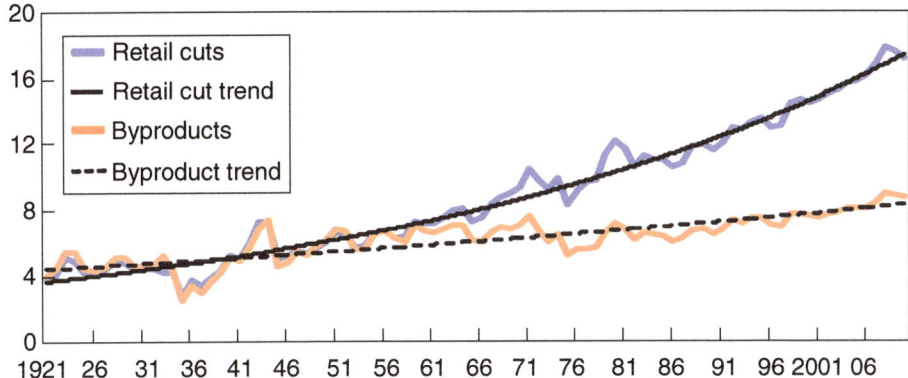

Source: USDA, Economic Research Service using data from USDA, National Agricultural Statistics Service; Ockerman and Hansen, 2000; and Aberle et al., 2001; and Ron Plain, University of Missouri.

Byproduct Values

Converting animal byproducts to useful goods with value has two effects. First, the meat industry captures additional revenue that otherwise would have been unrealized. Second, the costs of disposing of these secondary items are avoided. Intrinsically, animal byproducts serve as an extra means for packers to earn revenue or as a cushion to cover losses should the cost of purchasing the live animal exceed the selling price of the carcass.

In the last decade, live-equivalent hog prices have risen faster than carcass cutout values, which are the prices received by the packer. The hog carcass cutout value is an estimate of the value of a 51-52-percent lean, 185-pound hog carcass, based on wholesale prices being paid for subprimal pork cuts obtained from primal cuts, the basic major cuts into which carcasses and sides are separated. Pork primals include the loin, butt, picnic, sparerib, ham, belly, and jowl.

From 2000 to 2010, annual hog carcass cutout values rose by 27.7 percent (fig. 5). During the same period, however, the annual hog byproduct drop value increased by 80.3 percent. Currently, 2011 has had record-high year-to-date hog byproduct drop values. This allows packers to bid higher prices for live hogs than they might have in the absence of the value added from byproducts.

Figure 5
Prices and trends of U.S. live hog, carcass cutout, and byproduct values

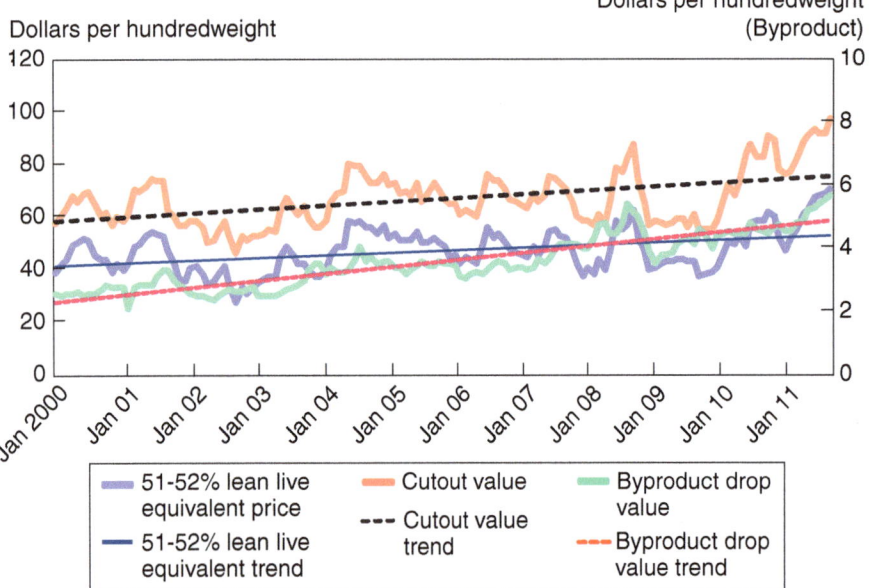

Source: USDA, Economic Research Service using data from USDA, Agricultural Marketing Service.

The importance of byproducts to livestock production can also be assessed by examining the proportion of value derived from wholesale byproduct sales in relation to the value generated from sales of total wholesale items produced from the animal. On a dressed-value basis, the total wholesale value of an animal can be defined as:

$$(TWv) = (COv) \times (COdw) + (BPv) \times (BPlw),$$

where TWv is the total wholesale value of an animal, COv is the weighted average cutout value of an animal's dressed carcass, $COdw$ is the cutout dressed weight of the animal's carcass, BPv is the byproduct drop value per live weight of an animal, and $BPlw$ is the live weight of the animal. Therefore, the portion of the animal's value derived from the byproduct value is at least:

$$\frac{BPv * BPlw}{Twv}.$$

This calculation may not reflect the full value of the animal derived from byproduct value because kidney fat (diaphragm fat) and certain bones trimmed off of the carcass and sold as byproducts are still attached when the dressed carcass is weighed. Therefore, one can say that *at least* this much value is added from byproducts. As a greater percentage of the total value gained from the animal is derived from the byproduct value, byproducts are becoming increasingly more valuable to livestock feeders, as packers are willing to bid higher prices for these animals. For 2000, an estimated 5.1 percent of annual packer earnings per hog came from byproduct sales. Although down from its high of 8.7 percent in 2009, the annual proportion of packer revenue earned per animal from byproducts was 7.0 percent in 2010, 36.7 percent above what was earned in 2000, which indicates that hog byproducts have grown in importance in packers' margins over time (fig. 6). This growth has important implications in the context of marginal profitability. Likewise, as the value of byproducts increases, all else remaining equal, the total value of live animals also increases.

Figure 6
Percent of value added to hogs from byproducts

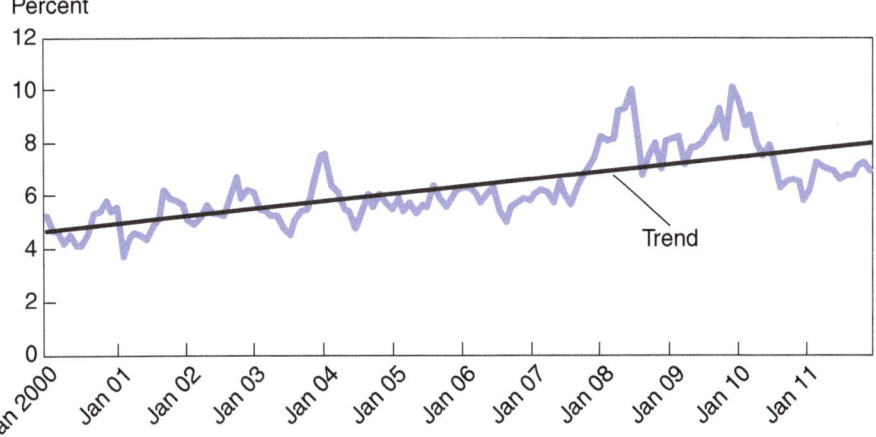

Source: USDA, Economic Research Service using data from USDA, Agricultural Marketing Service.

Numerous factors help account for the increase in byproduct values in recent years. Historically, byproducts were once more commonly consumed during meals, in addition to being used for a number of household products. Over time, cheaper synthetic materials were substituted in household products and labor and other costs associated with production and harvesting of byproducts rose, resulting in a decline in byproduct values. Further, U.S. immigrants and their descendants increasingly developed preferences for muscle cuts and other meat products, which also reduced demand for byproducts. More recently, however, a wider variety of uses and outlets for offal products has raised the value of these products relative to that of muscle cuts. The pet food industry, for example, has significantly boosted demand and, hence, value for animal byproducts. Common items found in retail store pet stores now include rawhide "bones," pizzles, joints and tendons, dry pet food made from processed offal, and pig ears, which are one of the most expensive parts of a hog carcass on a per weight basis.

Steer byproduct values, like those for pork, have increased since 2000, although not as significantly as pork byproducts. A sharp rise in foreign demand for swine offal in recent years, countered by a decline in demand for beef/veal offal, may account for the difference in growth rates. This may be because foreign demand for swine offal has risen quickly while bovine offal exports have fallen over the last few years, as discussed later in the trade section of this paper. The annual drop value of steer byproducts rose by 34.8 percent from 2000 to 2010, and similar to that for pork, beef carcass cutout prices also trended upward over the period. This study uses a weighted-average cutout value of Choice and Select cattle prices as an indicator for the prices received by the packer. This value simply accounts for the proportion of cattle slaughtered in each grade (Choice or better and Select) by the respective cutout value for each: a price calculated from the value of beef

Figure 7
Prices and trends of U.S. live steer, beef carcass cutout, and byproduct values

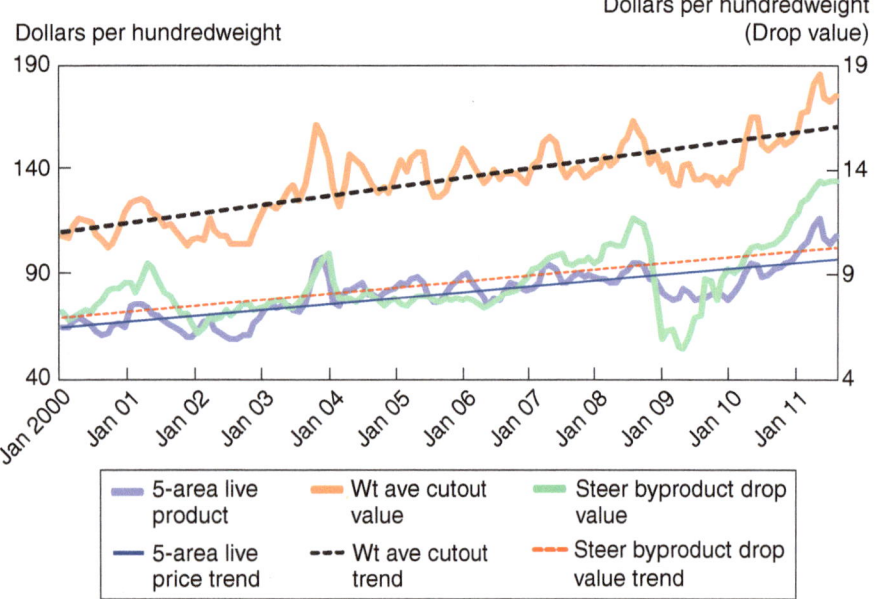

Source: USDA, Economic Research Service using data from USDA, Agricultural Marketing Service.

primal cuts, including ribs, chuck, round, loin, brisket, short plank, and flank. The weighted-average cutout value increased 36.4 percent from 2000 to 2010, an indication that packers are receiving, on average, over 36 percent more per carcass than they received a decade ago (fig. 7).

However, the five-area live steer price[2] trended upward by 38.1 percent during the same time period. Although it may seem counterintuitive that the live price rose faster than the cutout price given the drop value's slower growth, a 36.4-percent increase in the greater valued cutout price amounts to more on a per head basis than a 38.1-percent increase in the lesser valued live price. In this instance, a 41-cents-per-pound increase for weighted average cutout price is compared with a 26-cents-per-pound increase for the five-area live price. As with hog byproduct drop values, steer byproduct drop values for 2011 have also seen record high levels year-to-date.

As shown in figure 8, the annual average proportion of value added to a steer from byproducts remained virtually the same from 2000 to 2010, at 10.3 percent. However, from January to September 2011, the proportion averaged over 11 percent. Since a large share of byproduct value for cattle comes from hides, these values tend to follow hide values closely. For example, at the end of 2008, hide values plunged as effects of the worldwide recession dampened auto industry demand for leather and leather products.

Several factors help account for the sluggish growth in the value of beef byproducts relative to the value of the whole animal. Efficiency gains from technological advances have lowered the costs of recovering byproducts, enabling packers and renderers to sell more byproducts at a lower price and still maintain profitability. Also, technologies now exist for producing synthetic materials that replace byproducts, including synthetic materials to make items that were once made of leather, vegetable fats and oils to replace animal fats in cooking, synthetic detergents to replace soaps formerly made from animal fat, and cellulose sausage casings to replace casings made from intestines (Aberle et al., 2001).

[2]This price is listed as part of USDA, Agricultural Marketing Service's *5 Area Monthly Weighted Average Direct Slaughter Cattle – Negotiated* report (LM_CT180). It includes data from the Texas/Oklahoma/New Mexico; Kansas; Nebraska; Colorado; and Iowa/Minnesota feedlots. See www.ams.usda.gov/mnreports/lm_ct180.txt for the most recent report.

Figure 8
Percent of value added to the steer from byproducts

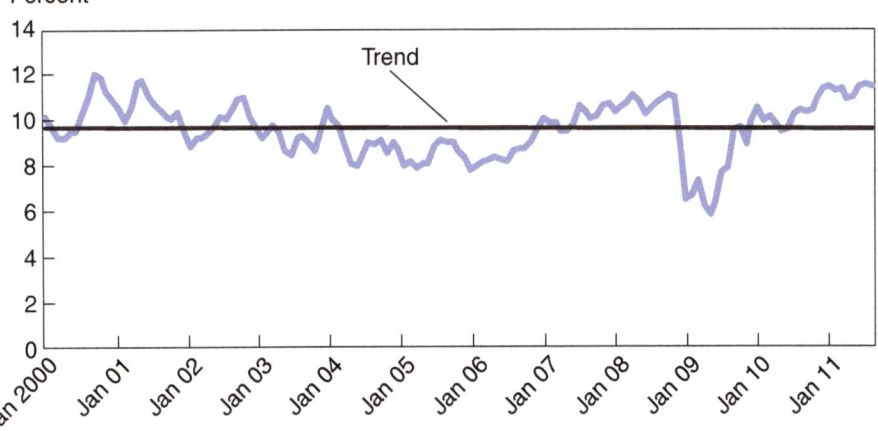

Source: USDA, Economic Research Service using data from USDA, Agricultural Marketing Service.

In addition, BSE affected byproduct markets in a number of ways and continues to restrict beef and beef/veal byproduct exports and export growth. For example, many countries imposed restrictions on imports of U.S. beef and variety meats: Mexico and South Korea banned imports of small intestines, China banned imports of beef and variety meats, Hong Kong banned imports of beef from cattle over 30 months of age, and Japan banned imports of beef and products from cattle over 21 months of age. Also, some products historically categorized as "edible" in certain countries are now classified as "inedible" (brains, spinal tissue, spinal cords, etc.) and, in some cases, are considered a biohazard.

Empirical Example of Determining the Contribution of Byproducts to Steer Prices

To gain a greater understanding of how byproducts add to the value of a steer, ERS developed ad hoc regression model estimates of the monthly weighted average, five-area steer prices for all grades of steers for the period January 2000 through July 2010. Model variables are outlined in appendix B. The estimate for the cattle byproduct drop value is positive and statistically significant, indicating that byproducts contribute positively to the value of live cattle. These findings suggest that a 10-percent increase in the byproduct drop value will result in a 1.1-percent increase in the five-area weighted average price for all grades of steers. For a full description of the methodology and findings of this model, see appendix B.

The carcass cutout value is statistically significant and positively contributes to live cattle value, whereas the number of head slaughtered is also statistically significant but negatively correlates with cattle prices. This indicates that shortages support cattle prices while surpluses depress them. The model shows that the effect of the BSE outbreak in Japan on cattle prices is negative but not significant. In fact, when BSE was discovered in Japan in September 2001, Japanese demand for beef fell, regardless of beef origin, which reduced foreign demand for U.S. beef and depressed steer prices. The effect on steer prices of the discovery of BSE in Canada is also significant and positive. This implies that when a case of BSE was found in Canada in May 2003, bans against imports of Canadian cattle affected U.S. domestic beef supplies, putting upward pressure on U.S. beef prices. Conversely, the effect of the U.S. BSE outbreak is negative, reflecting the decline in demand for U.S. beef when a case of BSE was found in a U.S. cow previously imported from Canada in December 2003.

Foreign Byproduct Price Comparison

To gain insight into the value of byproducts for U.S. packers and renderers, it is also useful to observe prices for the separate items that comprise the edible byproduct in both domestic and foreign markets. Tables 1 and 2 illustrate the difference in value for select products available in U.S., Chinese, and Mexican markets. All U.S. prices are weighted averages taken from the USDA, AMS *Pork and Beef Variety Meats Report*, and all foreign prices are converted to U.S. dollars.

Recent annual average prices for most of the variety meats are much higher than their 10-year averages, indicating that prices for these products are on the rise overall. Prices in the United States for some items, like stomachs, have trended upward in value closer to values in foreign markets. Greater international demand and higher prices for byproduct items add value to the live U.S. animal. As shown in the tables, certain U.S. items are particularly competitive in the Chinese and Mexican markets. While transportation costs, exchange rates, and tariffs all affect the costs of byproduct items imported from the United States, certain goods, such as kidneys, livers, hearts, tails, and tripe, cost more than twice as much in China than in the United States. Prices for these goods in Mexico, the closer of the two foreign markets, fall in between those in the United States and China.

Table 1
U.S.-Chinese-Mexican pork byproduct price comparison

Product	U.S. average price, 2000-2010	U.S. average price, 2010	U.S. price, week ending May 22, 2010	China price, May 20, 2010[1]	Central Mexico price, May 21, 2010[2]
			Dollars per hundredweight		
Kidneys	19.44	21.71	NA	146.11	NA
Livers	17.23	16.73	NA	51.80	NA
Ears	97.09	134.57	139.00	162.71	NA
Stomachs	65.23	106.85	112.00	112.90	NA
Chitterlings	42.41	NA	NA	83.01	NA
Hocks	29.06	42.73	37.00	69.73	NA
Hearts	33.84	32.47	33.00	89.66	NA
Tails	43.43	66.69	63.80	212.52	NA
Feet	34.97	46.85	51.00	83.01	57.69
Skins	25.00	40.00	NA	53.13	69.92
Tongues	75.97	135.30	122.00	136.14	NA
Head	NA	NA	NA	68.00	54.19
Cheek meat	66.17	93.48	94.70	NA	97.89
Visceras[3]	NA	NA	NA	NA	20.98

NA: Not applicable because these markets have not reported prices for these particular items during this time period.
[1]Chinese prices in terms of U.S. dollars use the exchange rate of 6.83 yuan to 1 dollar, as recorded by the Board of Governors of the Federal Reserve.
[2]Mexican prices in terms of U.S. dollars use the exchange rate of 12.974 pesos to 1 dollar, as recorded by the University of British Columbia Pacific Exchange Rate Service.
[3]An aggregated price for liver, heart, stomach, intestines, lungs, kidneys, and spleen sold in Aguascalientes, Mexico.
Source: USDA, Economic Research Service using data from USDA, Agricultural Marketing Service, LGMN Portal Database; Beijing Xinfadi Wholesale Market "price quotations" (translated by Fred Gale, ERS); and Sistema Nacional de Información e Intergración de Mercados.

Table 2
U.S.-Chinese-Mexican beef byproduct price comparison

Product	U.S. average price, 2000-2010	U.S. average price, 2010	U.S. price, week ending May 22, 2010	China price, May 20, 2010[1]	Central Mexico price, May 21, 2010[2]
			Dollars per hundredweight		
Kidneys	19.30	30.81	NA	53.24	NA
Tripe	43.59	49.06	NA	99.83	NA
Liver	25.89	54.16	NA	53.24	NA
Heart	28.91	47.08	NA	66.55	NA
Tongue	154.45	203.40	NA	133.10	NA
Visceras[3]	NA	NA	NA	NA	43.72

NA: Not applicable because these markets have not reported prices for these particular items during this time period.

[1]Chinese prices in terms of U.S. dollars use the exchange rate of 6.83 yuan to 1 dollar, as recorded by the Board of Governors of the Federal Reserve.

[2]Mexican prices in terms of U.S. dollars use the exchange rate of 12.974 pesos to 1 dollar, as recorded by the University of British Columbia Pacific Exchange Rate Service.

[3]An aggregated price for liver, heart, stomach, intestines, lungs, kidneys, and spleen sold in Aguascalientes, Mexico.

Source: USDA, Economic Research Service (ERS) using data from USDA, Agricultural Marketing Service, LGMN Portal Database; Beijing Xinfadi Wholesale Market "price quotations" (translated by Fred Gale, ERS); and Sistema Nacional de Información e Intergración de Mercados.

U.S. Edible Offal and the Global Marketplace

The supply of offal produced in the United States is much larger than its domestic demand. U.S. demand for edible offal stems mostly from use as ingredients in products such as sausages, hot dogs, and pet foods. Variety meats are more highly valued in foreign markets than in the United States. Exporting U.S. edible offal to markets with greater preferences for the products increases the overall value and profitability of the carcasses (Reed and Saghaian, 2004). Although carcasses and high-value cuts account for the majority of both volume and value of total U.S. red meat exports, edible offal exports constitute about 26 percent of the volume and about 15 percent of the value of total beef/veal- and pork-product exports over the last 5 years. The United States was historically the world's largest exporter of edible offal up until 2003. Although the United States is still the single largest exporter of edible offal, in 2004, the EU-27 as a region overtook the United States as the world's largest export trader of these products. Data from 2010 suggest that the United States supplies about 28 percent of the world's exports of edible offal for all species; the EU supplies about 36 percent (fig. 9). Still, the U.S. share is much less than what it was in the 1950s, when the United States accounted for 32 percent of world exports of edible offal (USDA-FAS, 1958).

Pork Edible Offal Exports and Markets

Exports of U.S. pork edible offal have steadily increased over the last two decades (fig. 10). The percentage of pork products exported from edible offal has averaged 22.5 percent annually over the last 5 years, as exports of U.S. pork edible offal have more than tripled from levels a decade earlier to almost 481,000 metric tons (MT)[3] in 2010. The 2010 exports were the largest

[3]One metric ton is approximately 2,204.6 pounds.

Figure 9
Major world edible offal exporting[1] countries by volume, 2010

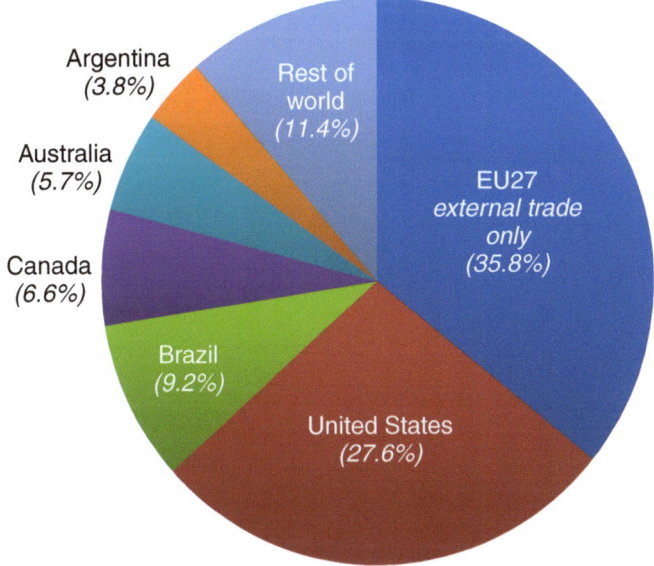

[1]Data include offal from bovine, swine, goats, and horses (HTS code sets 0206) and guts, bladders, and stomachs of animals other than fish (HTS code set 0504). At least 90 percent of these offal are of bovine and swine origin.

quantity of pork offal exports to date, accounting for 25 percent of the total volume of U.S. pork exports, the largest percentage in 6 years. In recent years, the value of U.S. exports of pork edible offal has also risen to historical highs. Prior to 2004, this amount was less than $200 million annually; it grew to $349 million in 2004 and has since more than doubled, reaching $708 million in 2008. In 2010, U.S. exports of pork edible offal were valued at $700 million, the third highest year on record.

Mexico is the largest importer of U.S. pork edible offal, accounting for over 42 percent of the U.S. exports over the last decade (fig. 11). Other major importers of U.S. pork edible offal include Hong Kong/China, Russia, Japan, and South Korea; however, many of these markets have developed only in the last 2-3 years. In this study, Hong Kong and China are grouped as one export destination. Hong Kong is more of an open market with fewer trade barriers, and as suggested by findings in another study, Hong Kong re-exports most of the pork edible offal imports to China (see Bean, 1996). In 2008, Hong Kong/China began to rival Mexico as the leading export market for U.S. pork edible offal in terms of volume. Until 2004, exports of all U.S. pork edible offal to Hong Kong/China were marginal; in 2008, they jumped to over 130,000 MT, close to a third of the U.S. total shipped worldwide. In 2010, Hong Kong/China became the number one export destination for U.S. exports of pork edible offal. With imports of 182,000 MT, or nearly 38 percent of total U.S. shipments, Hong Kong/China set a record among all countries. Prior to 2008, U.S. exports of pork edible offal to Russia were also minimal; however, in 2008, exports to Russia spiked at almost 61,000 MT, contributing to the near doubling of total U.S. exports of pork edible offal over the last few years of the decade. Offal can more easily be exported to Russia than muscle meat cuts because it does not fall under the tariff rate quotas that Russia imposes on other U.S. meats.

Major U.S. exports of pork edible offal in 2010 included fresh or chilled offal (13 percent of U.S. pork offal exports), hog feet (11 percent), rinds (8 percent), guts, bladders, and stomachs (8 percent), frozen intestines (7 percent) and all other frozen pork offal (45 percent) (fig. 12). Mexico imported 93 percent of

Figure 10
U.S. exports of swine meat and edible offal[1]

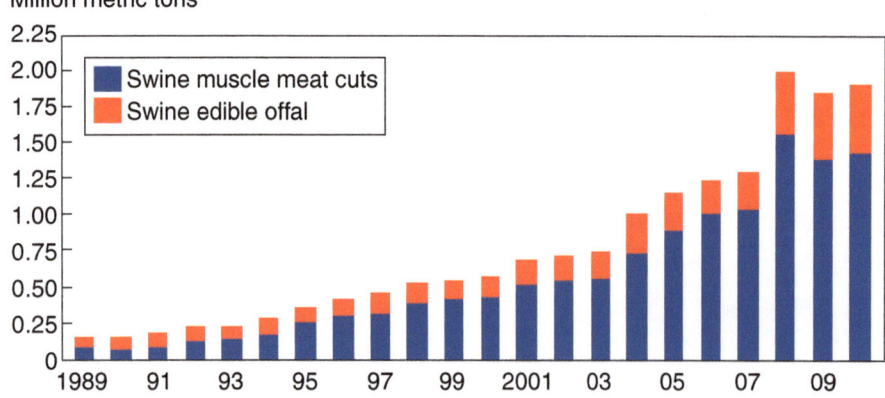

[1] Data include swine edible offal (HTS code sets 020630, 02064, 020649, 0504000020, 0504000080, and 16024910) and fresh, chilled, frozen, or prepared pork (HTS code sets 0203, 0210, 160241, 160242, 16024920, 16024940, and 16024970).
Source: USDA, Economic Research Service using data from USDA, Foreign Agricultural Service, Global Agricultural Trade System.

all U.S.-exported pork rinds, 93 percent of the prepared or preserved offal exports, and 65 percent of the fresh or chilled pork offal exports in 2010. Russia was the leading importer of U.S. swine head meat, and Hong Kong/China was the leading importer of U.S. hog feet, guts, stomachs and bladders, intestines, tongues, and pig hearts.

Figure 11
Top five export markets[1] for U.S. pork edible offal

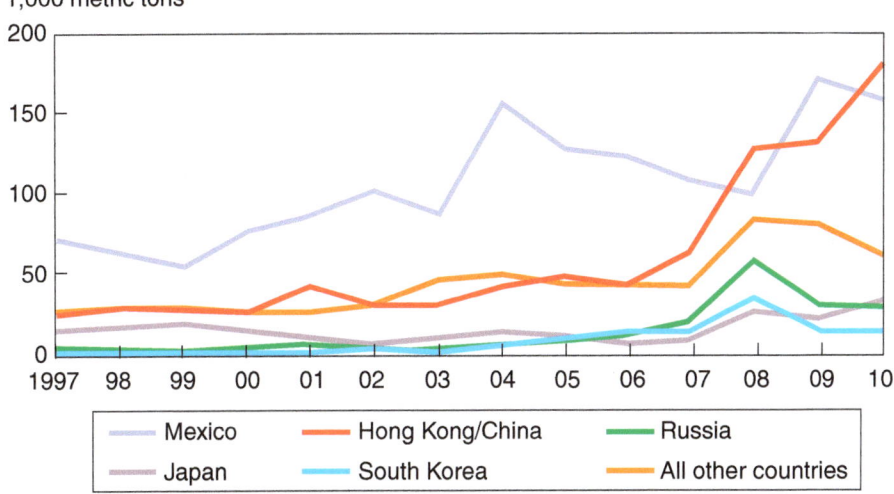

[1] These data include swine edible offal (HTS code sets 020630, 020641, 0504000020, 0504000080, and 16024910).
Source: USDA, Economic Research Service using data from USDA, Foreign Agricultural Service, Global Agricultural Trade Systems.

Figure 12
Top five export markets for U.S. pork edible offal by meat types,[1] 2010

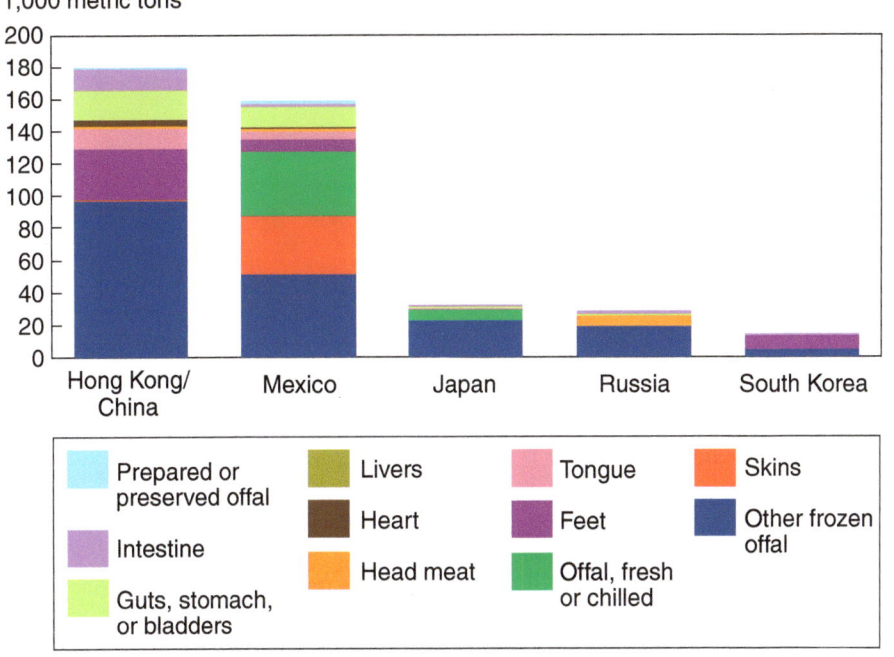

[1] These data include swine edible offal (HTS code sets 020630, 020649, 0504000020, 0504000080, and 16024910).
Source: USDA, Economic Research Service using data from USDA, Foreign Agricultural Service, Global Agricultural Trade System.

Beef Edible Offal Exports and Markets

U.S. exports of beef and veal edible offal have been steadily increasing since being disrupted by the BSE outbreak in 2003. In 2010, bovine meat exports from the United States were 89 percent of their 2003 levels, and bovine edible offal exports were 74 percent of their 2003 levels. Although edible offal's share of bovine product exports in the last 3 years has been less than the historical average, it reached almost 29 percent in 2009 (fig. 13). From 1990 to 2003, the average annual growth in the value of bovine edible offal exports was 10.7 percent, meaning that the value of bovine offal exported from the United States rose by over $413 million to $711 million during that period. After the initial decline of exports in 2004, the annual value of exports of U.S. bovine edible offal again climbed, reaching $541 million in 2010.

Historically, Japan was the largest importer of U.S. bovine edible offal, buying 32 percent of U.S. exports from 1997 to 2003. In Japan, items such as tongue, liver, stomach, and intestines are commonly used in barbecue, hot pot dishes, stews, and soups for both at-home and away-from-home consumption (Obara et al., 2010). Other traditionally large importers of U.S. bovine edible offal include Mexico, Egypt, Russia, and Canada (fig. 14). In these markets, "end cuts" and variety meats—the traditionally lower priced beef products in the United States—are bid away from competing uses in the United States. This contributes to an increase in the U.S. cutout value, and, ultimately, value is added to U.S. cattle at slaughter.

U.S. exports of bovine edible offal to major markets have increased gradually since 2003. During the same period and prior to the recent political turmoil in Egypt, U.S. exports of the product to Egypt also rose dramatically. In 2008, about 33 percent of U.S. exports of bovine edible offal went to Egypt, making it the largest destination for U.S. bovine variety meats that year (fig. 14). Having risen since 2006, U.S. exports to Egypt slowed in 2008-09 due in part to increased competition from Russia. Once Russia reopened its market to the United States, it started buying more U.S. beef livers, which drove up prices for Egyptian importers. However, a larger factor in the 2008-09

Figure 13
U.S. exports of bovine meat and edible offal[1]

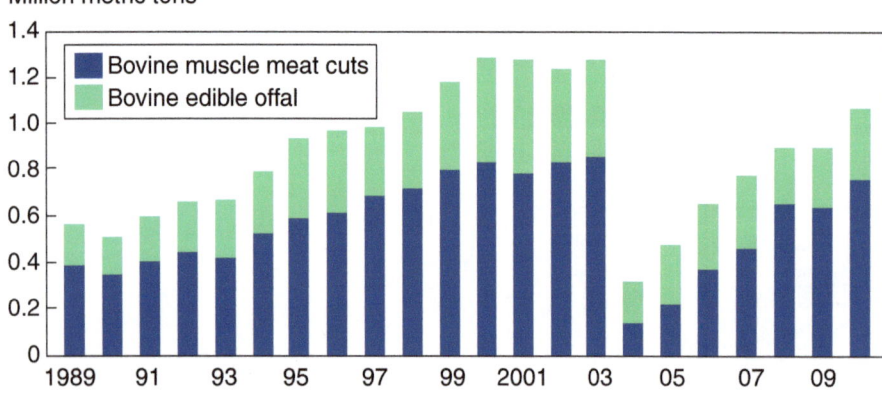

[1] Data include bovine edible offal (HTS code sets 020610, 020622, 0504000050, 0504000070), and fresh, chilled, frozen, or prepared bovine meat (HTS code sets 0201, 0202, 16024920, 1602509020, and 1602509500).
Source: USDA, Economic Research Service using data from USDA, Foreign Agricultural Service, Global Agricultural Trade System.

Figure 14
Top five export markets for U.S. bovine edible offal[1]

1,000 metric tons

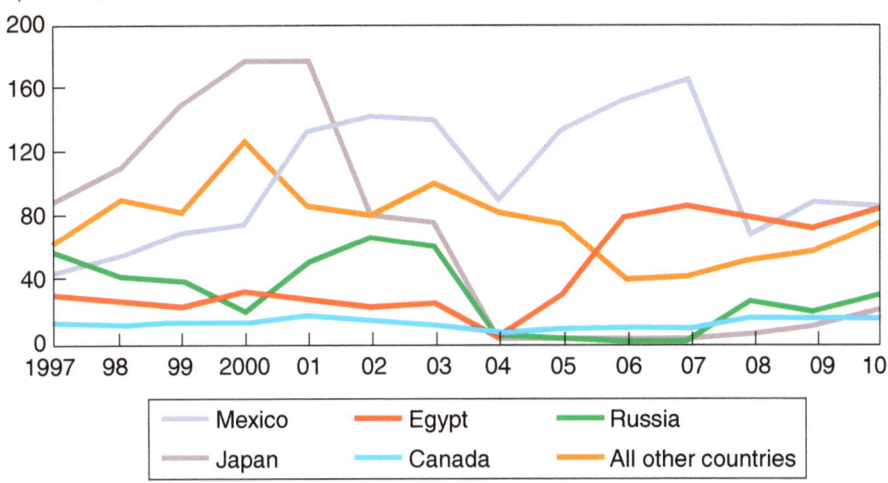

[1] These data include bovine edible offal (HTS code sets 020610, 020622, 020629, 0504000050, 0504000070).
Source: USDA, Economic Research Service using data from USDA, Foreign Agricultural Service, Global Agricultural Trade System.

slowdown may have been the global economic crisis, which resulted in tightened credit and a weakened Egyptian pound. In 2010, U.S. exports of bovine edible offal to Egypt almost recovered to their peak levels of 2007. The increase was driven by the efforts of Egyptian entrepreneurs who put beef liver and other price-competitive items in Egypt's retail outlets and supermarkets as well as on the menus of hotels and restaurants. Mexico currently remains the top export destination for U.S. bovine edible offal, if only by a small margin. In 2010, Mexico imported 87,700 MT of bovine edible offal from the United States, just 2,600 MT more than Egypt.

Traditionally, beef liver has been the top U.S. export of bovine edible offal. In 2010, bovine livers accounted for 31 percent of all U.S. exports of bovine edible offal (fig. 15). Other top U.S. exports of bovine edible offal include tripe (14 percent of U.S. edible offal exports) hearts (8 percent), tongue (5 percent), lips (4 percent), and all other frozen offal (29 percent). In 2010, 53 percent of all U.S. bovine liver exports went to Egypt, with another 21 percent going to Russia. Egypt also accounted for 35 percent of U.S. bovine kidney exports. In 2010, the majority of all U.S. exports of beef lips, sweetbreads, tripe, and tongue went to Mexico; more than half of U.S. exports of fresh or chilled bovine offal went to Japan; and about 28 percent of U.S. exports of all other frozen bovine offal went to Egypt, with Mexico taking the second highest volume.

Together, edible bovine and porcine byproducts accounted for more than 16 percent of the total value of U.S. bovine/porcine exports—which include edible offal and meat—over the last 10 years. In 2010, exports of pork and beef/veal edible offal accounted for only 14 percent of the total value of U.S. bovine/porcine exports, a lower-than-average share due to record-high export values of beef/veal and pork muscle meat. However, exports of beef/veal and pork edible offal in 2010 did reach a record $1.2 billion, $135 million more

Figure 15
Top five export markets for U.S. bovine edible offal by meat types,[1] 2010

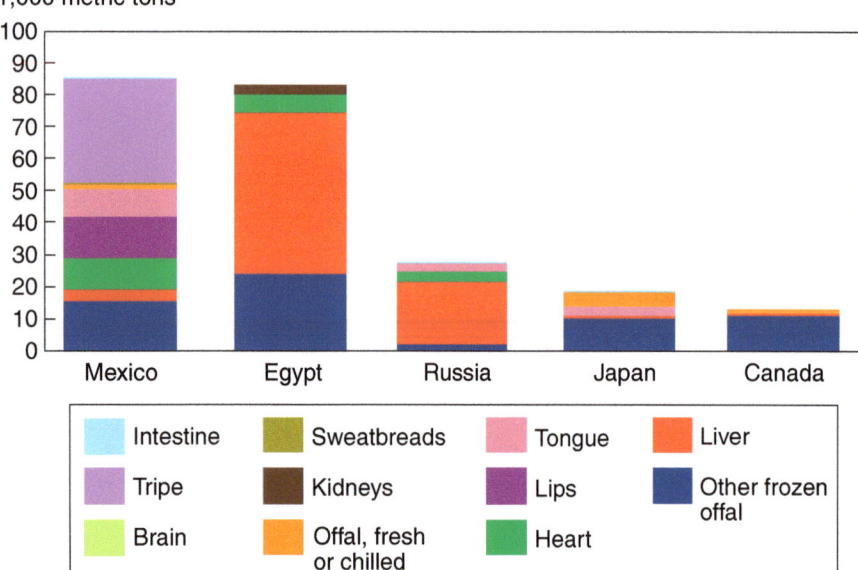

[1] These data include bovine edible offal (HTS code sets 020610, 020621, 020629, 0504000050, 0504000070).
Source: USDA, Economic Research Service using data from USDA, Foreign Agricultural Service, Global Agricultural Trade System.

Figure 16
Export value of U.S. bovine and porcine muscle meat and edible offal[1]

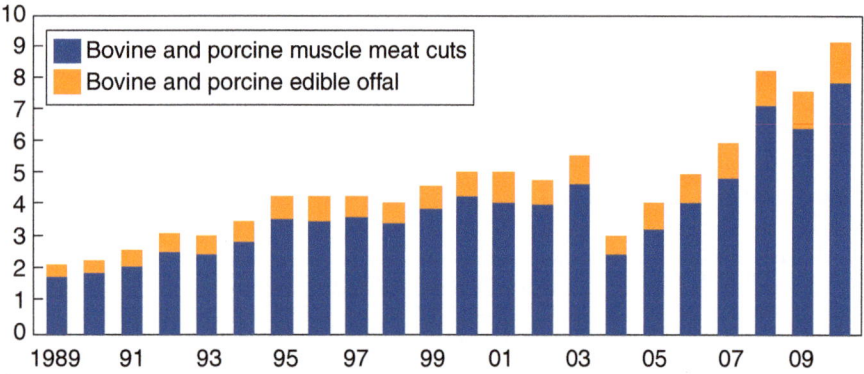

[1] Data include bovine and porcine edible offal (HTS code sets 020610, 020621, 020622, 020629, 020630, 020641, 020649, 0504000020, 0504000050, 0504000070, 0504000080, and 1602491000), and fresh, chilled, frozen, bovine and pork meat (HTS code sets 0201, 0202, 0203, 021011, 021012, 021019, 201020, 160241, 160242, 1602492000, 1602494000, 1602497000, and 160250).
Source: USDA, Economic Research Service using data from USDA, Foreign Agricultural Service, Global Agricultural Trade System.

than the previous high set in 2009. The U.S. export value of edible beef/veal and pork offal has increased every year since 2004 (fig. 16).

Total world imports of edible offal have increased significantly in recent years, and emerging markets for U.S. byproducts are evident. Currently, Hong Kong/China, Mexico, and Russia import the greatest shares of total

Figure 17
Historical top five world importers of edible offal[1] by volume

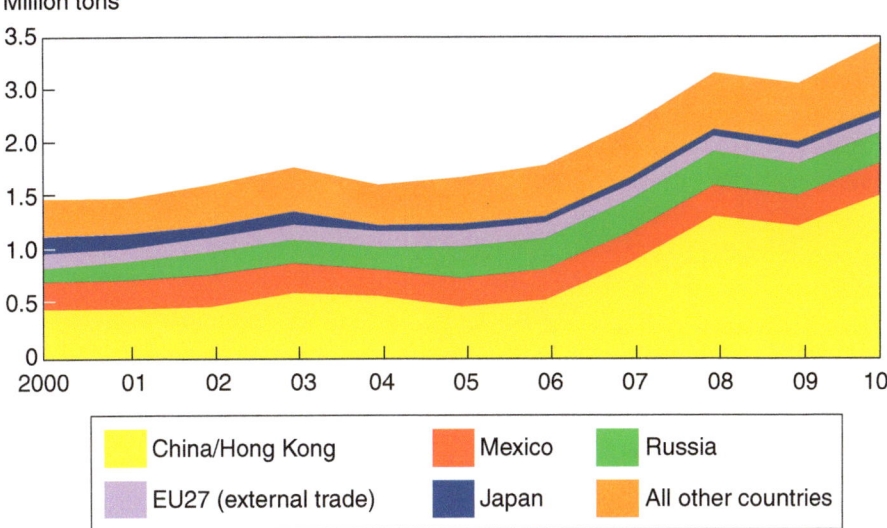

[1] Data include edible offal from bovine, swine, sheep, goats, and horses (HTS code sets 0206) and guts, bladders, and stomachs or animals other than fish (HTS code set 0504). At least 80 percent of these offal are of bovine and swine origin.
Source: USDA, Economic Research Service using data from Global Trade Information Services, Global Trade Atlas (complete data available only through 2009).

world exports of edible beef/veal and pork offal in terms of volume (fig. 17). Combined, these countries accounted for two-thirds of the world's edible offal imports over the last 10 years. Imports of beef/veal and pork edible offal by Hong Kong and China increased significantly during the period, mostly because of rising populations and swiftly growing incomes. Historically, the Philippines has not been a major importer of edible offal, but in 2010, the country almost doubled its annual total and overtook Japan as the world's fifth largest importer of edible offal.

Worldwide, the types of proteins consumed are often dependent upon peoples' income levels as well as cultural and religious practices. Increasing per capita incomes and rising GDP may have varied effects on consumption and trade of variety meats, depending on how the products are viewed in each country. In countries such as Egypt, where certain variety meats are popular, increasing wealth and GDP growth may result in increased U.S. variety meat exports. Egyptian demand for bovine products should remain strong in the coming years, especially since Egypt has a younger population, a relatively high rate of economic growth, and a limited capacity to expand domestic production (Kamenski, 2006). Variety meats are also highly valued in many Asian markets, where, in the long term, increases in U.S. meat and variety meat exports are anticipated. However, in portions of the Mexican and Russian markets, for example, where variety meats are less highly valued, variety meat consumption may give way to increasing consumption of muscle cuts as tastes and preferences change. While U.S. exports of variety meats could decline as incomes rise in some countries, preferences in other countries, such as China, for certain culinary traditions that are strongly tied to variety meat use will continue to play an integral role in demand for U.S. variety meat exports.

Conclusions

The many uses of animal byproducts are often overlooked; however, these items contribute a significant value to the U.S. livestock and meat industries. Uses for animal byproducts include, but are not limited to, certain industrial, household, and cosmetic products; livestock feed additives; pet foods; pharmaceutical and medical supplies; human consumption; and foreign exportation.

Although the development of synthetic substitutes in the middle of the 20th century decreased the value of many animal byproducts, recent use in the pet food industry and the medical field and rising export demand are contributing to an increase in byproduct values in recent years. Evidence of byproduct value appreciation can be seen in both the beef and pork industries, but only for pork has the proportion of value added to the hog from the byproduct value increased significantly over the last decade. Empirical analysis reveals that wholesale byproduct values marginally influence the live animal's value. This finding is supported by the willingness of packers to pay marginally more (or less) for live animals based on current byproduct market values.

Because the U.S. supply of edible offal typically exceeds domestic demand, the United States has historically been the world leader in exports of bovine and swine byproducts. Therefore, emerging markets that value offal products and are expanding their consumption will continue to play an important role in U.S. offal exports and thus, the U.S. livestock industry.

References

Aberle, E.D., J.C. Forrest, D.E. Gerrard, and E.W. Mills. *Principles of Meat Science*, Fourth edition, Kendall/Hunt Publishing Co.: Dubuque, IA, 2001.

Bean, R. "Beef Tongues to Pork Maws, Foreign Markets Hunger for Variety Meats," *AgExporter*, June-July 1996, http://findarticles.com/p/articles/mi_m3723/is_n5_v8/ai_18752623/?tag=content;col1

Beijing Xinfadi Wholesale Market. "Price Quotations," Translated by Fred Gale, U.S. Department of Agriculture, Economic Research Service, Accessed October 2010, www.xinfadi.com.cn/channel/13195963

Corbin, J.E. "Inedible Meat, Poultry and Fish By-Products in Pet Foods," in A.M. Pearson and T.R. Dutson (eds.), *Inedible Meat By-Products, Advances in Meat Research*, Vol. 8. pp, 329-347, Elsevier Applied Science: London, 1992.

Danilevici, C., M. Iordan, and M. Niã. "Valorisation of By-Products From Food Industry, Means of Effective Protecting the Environment," *Annals, Food Science and Technology*, 2009, www.afst.valahia.ro/anale2009/vol1/sectiunea4/10_CONSTANTIN_DANILEVICI_2.pdf

Duewer, Larry. "Updated Beef Carcass-to-Retail Consumption Conversion Factor Increases to 0.7," *Livestock Dairy and Poultry Outlook*, Outlook Report No. LDP-51, U.S. Department of Agriculture, Economic Research Service, May 1998, http://usda.mannlib.cornell.edu/usda/ers/LDP-M/1990s/1998/LDP-M-05-21-1998.txt

Dyck, J.H., and K.E. Nelson. *Structure of the Global Markets for Meat*, Agriculture Information Bulletin 785, U.S. Department of Agriculture, Economic Research Service, September 2003, www.ers.usda.gov/publications/aib785/

Franco, D.A., and W. Swanson. *The Original Recyclers*, Animal Proteins Producers Industry, Fats and Proteins Research Foundation, and National Renderers Association, 1996.

Goodlight, A. "Medical Breakthroughs: Pig Parts for the Human Body," *Associated Content from Yahoo*, August 18, 2010, www.associatedcontent.com/article/5684798/medical_breakthroughs_pig_parts_for.html?cat=58

Halstead, T. "U.S. Variety Meat Exports on the Upswing," *FAS online*, 1999, www.fas.usda.gov/dlp2/circular/1999/99-03LP/variety.htm

Hayes, Dermot. "Chinese Market for U.S. Pork Exports," *Trade Research Center*, August 1997, pg. 11, http://ageconsearch.umn.edu/bitstream/29173/1/pip02.pdf

Kamenski, C. "Variety Meats Vital to Boosting U.S. Beef Exports," *Issues Update*, March-April 2006, pp. 29-30, www.beefusa.org/uDocs/varietymeatsvitaltoexports.pdf

Marti, Daniel L., and Rachel J. Johnson. "Special Article: U.S. Variety Meat Exports and the Global Marketplace," in *Livestock, Dairy, and Poultry Outlook*, Outlook Report No. LDP-M-195, U.S. Department of Agriculture, Economic Research Service, September 2010, www.ers.usda.gov/publications/ldp/2010/09sep/ldpm195.pdf

Mathews, K.H. Jr. "Economic Impacts of Feed-Related Regulatory Responses to Bovine Spongiform Encephalopathy," in *Livestock, Dairy, and Poultry Outlook*, Outlook Report No. LDP-M-170-01, U.S. Department of Agriculture, Economic Research Service, September 2008, http://usda.mannlib.cornell.edu/usda/ers/LDP-M//2000s/2008/LDP-M-09-04-2008_Special_Report.pdf

Mathews, K.H. Jr., M. Vandeveer, and R.A. Gustafson. "An Economic Chronology of Bovine Spongiform Encephalopathy in North America," in *Livestock, Dairy, and Poultry Outlook*, Outlook Report No. LDP-M-143-01, U.S. Department of Agriculture, Economic Research Service, June 2006. http://usda.mannlib.cornell.edu/usda/ers/LDP-M//2000s/2006/LDP-M-06-09-2006_Special_Report.pdf

Mexico, Republic of, Secretaria de Economia. Sistema Nacional de Informacion e Integracion de Mercados website, Accessed October 2010, www.economia-sniim.gob.mx/Nuevo/

Murray, S.M., A.R. Patil, G.C. Fahey, Jr, N.R. Merchen, and D.M. Hughes. "Raw and Rendered Animal By-Products as Ingredients in Dog Diets," *Journal of Animal Science*, 1997, 75:2497-2505.

National Renderers Association. *Render*, Alexandria, VA, Various April issues.

Obara, K., M. McConnell, and J. Dyck. *Japan's Beef Market*, U.S. Department of Agriculture, Economic Research Service, Outlook Report No. LDP-M-194-01, August 2010, www.ers.usda.gov/publications/ldp/2010/08aug/ldpm19401/ldpm19401.pdf

Ockerman, H.W., and C.L. Hansen. *Animal Byproduct Processing and Utilization*, First edition, Lancaster, PA: Technomic, 2000.

Ockerman, H.W., and L. Basu. "Edible Rendering—Rendered Products for Human Use," April 29, 2010, https://dspace.lib.ohio-state.edu/dspace/bitstream/1811/45284/1/Rendering_Chapter.pdf

Pearl, G.G. "Animal By-Products: Biological and Industrial Products," in W.G. Pond and A.W. Bell (eds.), *Encyclopedia of Animal Science* 19-21, Marcel Dekker: New York, 2005.

Plain, R.L. Professor of Agricultural Economics, University of Missouri, Personal communication, October 27, 2010.

Prokop, W. H. "The Rendering Industry—A Commitment to Public Service," in *The Original Recyclers*, D.A. Franco and W. Swanson (eds.), pp. 17-21, Animal Protein Producers Industry, Fats and Proteins Research Foundation, National Renderers Association, 1996.

Reed, M. R., and S.H. Saghaian. "Measuring the Intensity of Competition in the Japanese Beef Market," *Journal of Agricultural and Applied Economics* 36(1): 113-121, April 2004.

U.S. Department of Agriculture, Agricultural Marketing Service. "LGMN Portals Database," http://marketnews.usda.gov/portal/lg

U.S. Department of Agriculture, Agricultural Marketing Service. *Market News Reports*, http://www.ams.usda.gov/AMSv1.0/ams.fetchTemplateData.do?template=TemplateB&navID=MarketNewsAndTransportationData&leftNav=MarketNewsAndTransportationData&page=LSMarketNewsPage

U.S. Department of Agriculture, Economic Research Service. *Weights, Measures, and Conversion Factors for Agricultural Commodities and Their Products*, Agricultural Handbook No. 697, 1992.

U.S. Department of Agriculture, Foreign Agricultural Service (a). "Foreign Agricultural Trade of the United States," www.fas.usda.gov/ustrade/

U.S. Department of Agriculture, Foreign Agricultural Service (b). *United States Variety Meats in World Markets*, FAS M-43, October 1958.

U.S. Department of Commerce, U.S. Bureau of the Census. *Current Industrial Report, M311K—Fats and Oils, Production Consumption, and Stocks*, Various issues.

Appendix A — Types of Offal by Category

Appendix table A-1
Types of offal by category

Category	Raw byproduct	Principal use
Edible offal	Brain	Variety meats
	Head meat	Sausage ingredients, variety meats
	Heart	Variety meats
	Kidneys	Variety meats
	Liver	Variety meats
	Spleen (melt)	Variety meats
	Stomach (tripe)	Cheese making components, sausage components, variety meats
	Tail	Variety meats
	Testicles (fries)	Variety meats
	Thymus or pancreas (sweetbreads)	Variety meats
	Tongue	Variety meats
Inedible/edible offal	Blood	Adhesives, ceramics, cosmetics, feed use, fertilizer, foam in fire extinguishers, insecticides, laboratory use, medical use, plastics, sausage components
	Bones	Animal feed, buttons and handles, capsules for medications, cosmetics, emulsions, fertilizer, gelatins, glues, hardening steel, candies and dairy products, ointments, paper, photographic films, refining sugar, textiles
	Connective tissue	Gelatins
	Ears	Pet food, variety meats
	Fats	Candies, chewing gum, germicides, industrial oils, insecticides, lubricants, soap, glycerin, medicinal products, shortenings, tires
	Feet	Fine lubricants, leather preparations, variety meats
	Intestines (chitterlings or natural casings)	Sausage components, variety meats, medical use
	Skin	Candies, capsules for medications, cosmetics, dairy products, emulsions, gelatins, leather goods, ointments, paper, photographic films, rinds, textiles
Inedible offal	Glands	Industrial products, medicines
	Hair	Athletic equipment, brushes, felt, insulation, rugs, upholstery
	Hide	Boxes and plywood, gelatins, glues, leather goods
	Lungs	Pet foods

Source: USDA, Economic Research Service using data from Aberle et al., 2001; Ockerman and Hansen, 2000; Pearl, 2005; Goodlight, 2010; Corbin, 1992; and Murray et al., 1997.

Appendix B — Steer Byproducts Model

To gain a greater understanding of how byproducts contribute to the value of a steer, we estimated an ad hoc regression model of the monthly weighted average, five-area steer prices for all grades of steers for January 2000 through December 2011. The log-log model specification facilitates the interpretation of the parameters as response parameters or a form of elasticity.

Variables used in the regression model are outlined in appendix table 1. A weighted average of Choice and Select cutout values is calculated to represent all grades. Cutout values, byproduct values, prices for 50-percent trim, and hog prices were originally from USDA, Agricultural Marketing Service reports. Data on total federally inspected cattle slaughter come from USDA, National Agricultural Statistics Service *Livestock Slaughter*. Data on live cattle imports are obtained from ERS web sources. Indicator variables for bovine spongiform encephalitis (BSE) confirmations in export markets important to the United States are constructed based on BSE confirmation dates. Trigonometric variables were added to account for seasonality and any effects from the cyclical nature of cattle inventories.

Any extra products from an animal would generally be expected to add value to the animal, meaning that they would have a positive effect on steer prices. This is the case in the model for cutout, byproduct, and trim values, although only the effects from cutout and byproduct values are statistically significant. The price of a substitute, hogs in this case, is also expected to be positive as it is in this model, but, again, not statistically significant.

Interpretation of the byproduct parameter—the main parameter of interest in this model—is that a 1-percent increase in byproduct values results in a 0.11-percent increase in steer prices. An increase in byproduct values from $13.20 to $13.33 (a 1-percent increase) implies an increase in the five-area steer price from $115.00 to $115.13 (a change in the steer price of 0.11 percent). Other parameters have similar interpretations but differ in magnitude and direction because of the signs attached to the parameter estimates.

Total federally inspected cattle slaughter, a quantity variable, was expected to have a negative effect on steer prices since, from a demand perspective, a larger quantity of the commodity would sell at a lower price. In this model, the sign for slaughter is negative and significant. The effect of a trade-related variable is not so easily explained. Imports of live cattle were expected to have a negative effect on U.S. steer prices because more cattle would sell at lower prices. However, the study is one in which cattle inventories were generally declining. Also, most of the imported cattle are feeder cattle, and a positive parameter may indicate demand for inputs into future production in the face of inadequate current supplies. The parameter for cattle imports is both positive and significant.

The indicator variable for BSE in Japan is negative but not significant, likely reflecting the adverse reaction of Japanese consumers to their own BSE events. The reluctance of Japanese consumers to consume any beef reduced exports of U.S. beef, and Japan was the top U.S. beef export market prior to their BSE confirmation. The U.S. BSE confirmation had an expected negative effect on steer prices but, interestingly, is not significant. U.S. prices for beef and cattle had been at record levels until October 2003 when they began declining. While initial responses were negative during the first couple weeks after the December 2003 U.S. BSE event, the effect was short lived, and U.S. consumers did not respond to the domestic BSE cases as adversely as consumers in other countries responded to their earlier BSE discoveries. The Canadian BSE variable was significant and had an expected positive effect on U.S. steer prices because reduced imports from Canada decreased domestic U.S. beef supplies, especially at a time when U.S. supplies were already low.

F-tests for seasonal and cyclical variables were not found to be significant. This was somewhat surprising because of the appearance of seasonality in the price series and results from other studies. However, seasonality exists in other variables, and it may be that the other variables captured the seasonal components, making seasonal variables redundant. The same is likely true for cyclical variables as well.

Appendix table B-1

Regression of weighted average five-area steer prices onto byproduct values and selected other variables, January 2000-July 2010

Variable	Description	Coefficient	Significance	t-Statistic
LOG(PR5AREASTEER)	Dependent variable: natural logarithm of 5-area weighted average price for all grades of steers sold on a negotiated basis, $/cwt			
C	Intercept	1.214785		1.763885
LOG(PRCHSELCUTOUT)	natural logarithm of weighted average Choice and Select cutout values, $/cwt	0.774930	***	12.32470
LOG(PRBYPROD)	natural logarithm of byproduct (drop) value, $/cwt	0.113227	***	5.094476
LOG(PR50TRIM)	natural logarithm of 50-percent lean trim, $/cwt	0.003789		0.297329
LOG(PRHOGS)	natural logarithm of prices for slaughter barrows and gilts, $/cwt	0.030727		1.044437
LOG(QFISLAU)	natural logarithm of Federally inspected cattle slaughter, million head	-0.096641	**	-2.365011
LOG(CATIMP)	natural logarithm of live cattle imports, million head	0.035176	***	4.859475
BSEJAPAN	dummy variable: 0 = before September 2001, 1= September 2001 and beyond	-0.014440		-1.417485
BSEUS	dummy variable: 0 = before January 2004, 1= January 2004 and beyond	-0.003648		-0.202876
BSECAN	dummy variable: 0 = before May 2003, 1=May 2003 and beyond	0.046636	***	2.680094
r-square = 0.962392				
F-statistic = 232.2765				

Significance levels are *** = 1% and ** = 5%
Source: USDA, Economic Research Service.

www.ingramcontent.com/pod-product-compliance
Lightning Source LLC
Chambersburg PA
CBHW041306180526
45172CB00003B/992